HOW TO LOOK AFTER YOUR

PET RABBIT

A PRACTICAL GUIDE TO CARING FOR YOUR PET, IN STEP-BY-STEP PHOTOGRAPHS

DAVID ALDERTON

ARMADILLO

Introduction

Rabbits can make great pets, but will you be prepared to look after one properly? Even when the weather is wet and cold, a pet rabbit living in its hutch in your garden will depend on you to give it fresh food and clean water. It will also need to be cleaned out each week. In the case of a house rabbit kept indoors, you must still look after your pet every day. You will have to spend money buying food and bedding regularly. Rabbits can live for a long time, for six or even ten years, so you must be fully prepared before you decide to buy a rabbit.

The tall ears of rabbits, and their short tail, mean they are always easy to recognize.

A caring owner

Your pet rabbit needs much more than being shut away in a hutch with food and water. It must be picked up and made a fuss of, as well as being allowed to run around in the home or in a safe part of the garden. You should also groom your pet regularly, and check its nails have not grown too long.

A young rabbit will become very friendly if you handle it often from an early age.

A rabbit will need a home called a hutch, which should be cleaned out at least once a week.

Family pet

You may have a brother or sister who likes the idea of having a rabbit, too. This means that you can both enjoy keeping a rabbit, and you can share the work of looking after your pet between you. This makes it much easier! Rabbits often prefer to live together, so choose two if you can – but you need to be sure that they will not have babies, and will not fight. Young rabbits are more likely to become friends than older ones. Rabbits are fun for all the family, but if you also have a dog or cat, then you must always keep them well away from your rabbit. Not only will they frighten a rabbit, but they may also hurt your pet.

Rabbits can run off very fast if they become frightened, so always be gentle and quiet so that your pet does not become scared.

Bolts are the safest way of keeping the doors of a hutch closed.

In a happy home

Rabbits can be kept either outdoors or indoors. They are quiet animals, so a pet rabbit won't disturb you if they live in your home, nor do they smell. This means that, even if you don't have a garden, it is still possible for you to keep a pet rabbit in your house. Most rabbits live in wooden cages, known as hutches. You can make your pet rabbit's hutch into a special home, by decorating the outside. There are also special runs that can be used to house your rabbit indoors. Choose the largest one you can.

What is a rabbit?

The first thing you notice about a rabbit is its long ears. These allow sounds to be heard easily, warning of possible danger. Rabbits that live in the wild face many dangers, as they are hunted on the ground by foxes and from the air by birds of prey. They need to be able to hide easily so that they can escape from their predators. This is why wild rabbits usually live in underground burrows, called warrens. They only come out of these tunnels to search for food when it appears to be safe.

Rabbits have very good hearing, thanks to their large ears. They have big eyes, too, so they can also see extremely well.

Relatives of rabbits

Rabbits are part of a large group of animals called mammals, which have fur or hair on their bodies and feed their young on milk. Rabbits and their relatives are sometimes called lagomorphs. Rabbits are similar to hares, which also have long ears, and pikas, whose ears are much smaller, although their body shape still looks like that of a rabbit.

There are more than 65 types of wild rabbits, hares and pikas found around the world. From one of these, the European rabbit, all of today's pet rabbits are descended – there are now more than 100 different breeds.

Looking around

When you look at a rabbit, you will notice its large eyes. Rabbits are able to see well, almost right around their heads. Their long, strong, muscular back legs mean they can also run away very fast, escaping from danger down their burrows. Rabbits have a very short tail, known as a bobtail. The white fur underneath the tail shows up very clearly when the rabbit is running, as it holds its tail up.

Rabbits will sometimes stand up on their back legs to see what is happening around them.

Show rabbits sometimes wear a ring. Check that this does not become too tight on your pet's leg. Your vet will need to remove it otherwise.

strong back legs

bobtail

Teeth, whiskers and noses

Rabbits feed on plants and vegetables. They have two very strong teeth in each jaw at the front of their mouths. These teeth are called incisors and allow rabbits to nibble off pieces of food easily. If you look more closely at each side of your rabbit's face, you will see long hairs known as whiskers. These are thicker than other hairs, and are sensitive, so they help the rabbit to find its way through gaps or along its burrow in the dark. Rabbits also have a good sense of smell – watch how their noses twitch, picking up scents in the air that could reveal a hidden danger.

Rex rabbits have very short, soft, cuddly coats, which feel nice to touch.

whiskers

nose

mouth

Rabbit varieties

There are now over 100 breeds of rabbit, which differ from each other in the way they look, just like breeds of dog do. Some rabbits are much bigger than others, while a number have long coats, which need more grooming than those with short coats. The Angora rabbit has very long fur, so it needs a lot of regular grooming – otherwise its fur becomes matted. Rex rabbits, with their short, soft coats, need less grooming. You can find Rex rabbits of various different sizes and colorations.

The fur of the Angora rabbit is often spun to make a very soft wool.

The Netherland Dwarf and its close relative, called the Polish, are very lively rabbits.

Netherland Dwarf rabbits

Certain breeds of rabbit are rare and may only be seen at large rabbit shows. The rabbits listed here are all very popular though, and will make good pets. The Netherland Dwarf is the smallest rabbit, which weighs about the same as a bag of sugar. Its ears are short, being about the same length as an adult's little finger. These rabbits have been bred in a wide range of shades, such as pure white and lilac, as well as patterns such as tortoiseshell, so there are plenty of varieties to choose from.

Lop Ears

This breed of rabbits varies in size, with the smallest being the Mini Lop. You can spot a lop rabbit very easily, because its ears hang down over the sides of its head, although in young lops this does not happen until they are about four weeks old. Lops are really friendly rabbits. They are less likely to kick than other breeds when picked up.

Smaller lops, which have been bred in a wide range of shades, are a good choice as pets, because they are easy to pick up.

Dutch rabbits

These rabbits make good pets. They are slightly bigger than the Netherland Dwarf, and about twice as heavy. Dutch rabbits always have white and darker areas of fur on their bodies. Their white area of fur extends around the shoulders, down under the chin and up between the eyes.

You can recognize Dutch rabbits by the unusual pattern of their white areas of fur.

The English breed has dark spots on its white body, dark ears and nose and a stripe down its back.

English rabbits

Some breeds have markings on their coats, like this English rabbit, which are very important if you want your rabbit to appear in shows. Each of these rabbits has its very own pattern of dark spots on its mainly white fur. They are very friendly animals too.

Big rabbits like the British Giant are very friendly but are heavy to pick up. They can sometimes have dark coats, too.

British Giants

There are even larger breeds than the Dutch rabbits, with some, like the British Giant rabbit, being as big as a small dog. This means that when fully grown these rabbits are heavy, and so will be more difficult for you to pick up easily and safely on your own.

Choosing your rabbit

When you are looking for a pet, it's important to find a rabbit that is around six weeks old. At this stage, the young rabbit has just left its mother, and it will be easy for you to make friends with it. Older bunnies are likely to be less friendly, unless they have become used to being picked up and being handled regularly by their previous owner.

It's hard choosing a pet rabbit as they all look so cute. These are baby Dutch rabbits.

Where to go

There are several places where you can go to find a pet rabbit. Pet stores often have a good choice, but if you want a special breed, you may have to look for a breeder in your area.

Ask an adult to help you search on the Internet, or look in a newspaper or a magazine where breeders often advertise. You may have to wait if you want a particular breed or coloration, until a young rabbit is available. Alternatively, there are bunny rescue organizations in some areas, which sometimes have young rabbits that need a loving home.

If you go to a breeder, you may have to wait until your rabbit is old enough to come home with you.

One or two?

Most people have a single rabbit. If you want two to live together, you will need a very large cage, and you must also discover the gender of your rabbits, which is not always easy when they are still young. Two female rabbits, which are known as does, are the best. The males, called bucks, are more likely to fight, and if you have one of each they will breed.

Think carefully about what type of rabbit you want. Both the Rex (left) and Dutch are friendly breeds.

Bright and healthy

It is important when choosing a rabbit to look for any signs of illness. You can tell a lot about the health of a rabbit just by its appearance. A healthy rabbit will have bright eyes and a glossy coat, and when awake will be generally lively and alert.

The ears must be clean.

The coat should be glossy.

Check the eyes are bright.

Look at the teeth.

No staining under the tail.

Teeth

One of the the most important things to check with a rabbit is the incisor teeth at the front of its mouth. These must meet correctly, so there is no overhang or undershoot (where the teeth don't meet together properly), which would result in the teeth becoming overgrown. This will stop the rabbit eating, if they are not cut back regularly. Unlike our teeth, the incisors of rabbits continue growing throughout their lives, but are worn down as the rabbit nibbles its food.

Going home

When you go to collect your rabbit, take a secure, well-ventilated carrier with you, so you can bring your new pet home safely. Make the carrier as cosy as possible by lining the inside with newspaper or hay as bedding. This will make your rabbit comfortable on the journey.

Line the base of a cardboard carrier with a thick layer of newspaper or hay and always hold it underneath.

9

Your rabbit's home

Rabbits are active by nature and need plenty of space, so provide your rabbit with a good-sized hutch to live in. The hutch must also be tall enough to allow your pet to sit up easily. There are many different designs available, but most hutches are divided into two parts, one of which is opened by a mesh door. The other has a solid door, which provides your pet with somewhere safe to hide, rather like a burrow.

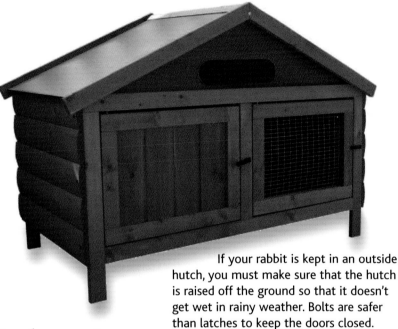

If your rabbit is kept in an outside hutch, you must make sure that the hutch is raised off the ground so that it doesn't get wet in rainy weather. Bolts are safer than latches to keep the doors closed.

In the garden

Outdoor hutches need strong legs, so they can stand on the ground without the bottom of the hutch becoming wet. If your hutch does not have legs, you could place it on a table or on a pile of bricks to raise it off the ground. The top of the hutch must be covered in roofing felt, to keep out the rain.

Where to put the run

It is not a good idea to let your pet loose in the garden, even if it is well-fenced. You can allow your rabbit out into a run on the lawn. The run should be in a shady position, as rabbits can die if left in direct sunlight. Your pet must have drinking water available, and there should be a sheltered area in the run, in case it starts raining. Make sure that the grass under the run hasn't recently been treated with weedkiller as this could harm your pet.

A typical rabbit run has a large door so you can catch your pet inside easily. A wire mesh buried beneath the turf prevents your pet from digging its way out.

Bedding

You will need safe, untreated wood shavings to line the floor of the hutch, with hay on top, which provides both bedding and a snack for your pet. Always buy fresh hay, and store it somewhere dry, so it will not become rotten. Never use sawdust instead of wood shavings as it is very fine, and could get into your rabbit's eyes, making them sore and irritated.

Hay is important for your rabbit to eat and also as bedding.

Wood shavings are used to line the floor of your rabbit's hutch.

House rabbits

Rabbits that live indoors in the home are often called house rabbits. It is possible to train them to use a litter box – just like a cat does. You will need to buy a low-sided litter box and some litter. Stand the box on several sheets of newspaper, and encourage your rabbit to start using it by tipping some droppings on to the box. Soon, your rabbit should be using the litter box regularly.

Once your rabbit has learned to use a litter box, it should not soil around the home.

Dangers in the home

You must check that your home is safe for a pet rabbit. Rabbits like to gnaw things, so keep flexes out of your pet's reach, behind furniture. Carpets too can be a problem, as some rabbits will nibble at them, and may swallow the fibres. Poisonous house plants must also always be out of the rabbit's reach.

Rabbits love to chew, but this can cause damage and may be dangerous for your pet.

Feeding

Rabbits are herbivores, which means they feed on plants and seeds in the wild. You can buy fresh and packeted foods for them at many supermarkets as well as pet stores, so feeding your rabbit, even if you do not have a garden, will not be difficult.

Dried food

This type of food often contains various seeds and dried grasses, as well as pellets. There may be flaked corn (maize) as well, which looks rather like cornflakes, plus alfalfa, a plant related to the pulse family, which look dark green. You may also see whole pieces of yellow corn, crushed dry peas and herbs. Rabbit foods also usually have all the vitamins and minerals needed to keep your pet healthy added to them, as part of the pellets. Pour dried food for your rabbit into a heavyweight feeding bowl that it will not be able to tip over. Avoid plastic food bowls because these are likely to end up being badly chewed by your pet. You may also want to give your pet occasional treat foods, sold in packets – and don't forget chews, which will help to keep its teeth trim.

Dried food

There are special treats that you can give your rabbit occasionally, but you should not use these instead of regular food.

Fill up the food bowl twice each day. Rabbits often feed after dark, so make sure that they have something to eat at night.

Your rabbit will not be able to tip over a heavy food bowl, nor will it be able to damage it with its teeth.

Fresh food

Always try to offer your rabbit some fresh food every day, although it is best not to change its diet suddenly, as this can lead to your pet having an upset tummy. Rabbits enjoy fruits and vegetables, such as cabbage, apples and peeled carrots but avoid offering them lettuce, as this does not always agree with them. You can also collect fresh foods from your garden, such as dandelion leaves and flowers. Some plants are poisonous though, especially bulbs, so only choose those that you know are safe for your rabbit to eat.

Wash all fresh food thoroughly and shake the water off before giving it to your pet. Don't offer too much fresh food and make sure you always throw away any that is left uneaten at the end of the day. You also need to be sure that your pet has enough hay to eat, as this provides valuable roughage in its diet.

You can give your rabbit a choice of fresh food. Be sure to wash and peel fruit and vegetables as necessary.

Water

Rabbits need fresh water every day. Buy a special drinking bottle, which can be fixed to the front of its cage, so your pet can drink easily from the spout. Take care not to place the drinking bottle above the food bowl, as it may drip into the food.

Your rabbit's drinking bottle can be attached to the mesh on the side of the hutch with a clip.

Rabbits enjoy eating fresh foods such as cabbage, which is full of healthy nutrients.

Handling

Start to pick up your new pet regularly from an early stage. Rabbits soon become used to being handled, and stop struggling. It is always best to wear long-sleeved clothes if you are going to pick up your rabbit, as their claws are sharp and could scratch your bare arm. This may cause you to drop your pet, which could injure it badly.

Always hold food so that your rabbit can take it easily from your hand.

Taming

One of the best ways to tame a rabbit is to offer it pieces of green food by hand. Although at first your rabbit may be shy about feeding in this way, it will soon learn to come to you for food. Just take care to let go at the right time so you don't get nipped by its teeth!

Picking up your rabbit

Before picking up your rabbit, make sure that if you have a dog, it is safe elsewhere in your home. Otherwise, the dog could frighten your pet if it jumps up at you. Then open the cage to pick up your rabbit.

1 Place one hand gently around the rabbit's neck, behind the ears.

2 Next, slide your other hand under its body so you are supporting its hindquarters.

3 Slip your first hand down behind the front legs to lift your rabbit up safely.

Carrying your rabbit

If you want to carry your rabbit anywhere, tuck it safely against your body. Rest it along your arm, so that its hindquarters are well-supported, as it is less likely to put up a struggle in this position and it is comfortable for you and your rabbit.

Putting your pet back

When you put your rabbit back into its hutch, do not encourage it to jump down, because it could hurt its back as a result. When you place it on the floor of the hutch, turn your face away because your pet may kick back with its hind feet at this stage.

It is very important that your rabbit does not accidentally fall on to the ground. A fall is likely to cause a serious back injury.

If a rabbit feels comfortable when it is being carried, then it will not struggle.

Careful handling

Never grasp your rabbit tightly or try to pick it up by holding its ears, as this will be very painful for your pet. It will be better to ask an adult to help you at first, so that you can see exactly what to do. Always take great care when handling big rabbits, because they will be a lot stronger and heavier than smaller ones.

Cleaning the hutch

Rabbits are very clean creatures, and they usually only soil in one corner of their hutch. If you have a small shovel, you can scoop out your pet's droppings every two or three days, cleaning the hutch thoroughly once a week.

Removing your rabbit

When you are cleaning out your rabbit's hutch, it will be safer to move your pet elsewhere. Put it in an outdoor run if the hutch is outside, or let your rabbit run around in the home, if it usually lives there. Or you can put your rabbit in its carrier, to be certain that it will be safe.

Sweeping the hutch

Take out the food bowl and put it somewhere safe. Wearing gloves, remove the old hay and shavings and put them into a plastic sack. Sweep out the hutch. You can tip the soiled bedding on to a garden compost heap.

If you take your rabbit out first, the hutch will be easier to clean.

Remove the old bedding first, into a sack. Wear gloves because this is a dirty task.

With a dustpan and brush you can easily sweep the floor of the hutch clean.

Washing the hutch

When the weather is warm and fine, wash out the hutch with the help of an adult, using a safe disinfectant and scrubbing brush. You should do this about three or four times a year or whenever it needs doing. Rinse off the inside of the hutch and allow it to dry thoroughly before putting in new bedding. The food bowl must be washed every week and dried with a paper towel before refilling it. You can clean the inside of the drinking bottle with a bottle brush.

Be sure to clean the food bowl thoroughly every week, tipping away the old food, and then dry it with a dry cloth.

Clean the drinker every week, too. A bottle brush will make this task much easier.

Only wash out the hutch on a warm day. A rabbit may develop a chill if put into a wet home.

Watch for flies

It is vital to keep the hutch clean, especially in the summer, as otherwise flies will be attracted to it. If your rabbit's fur becomes soiled with droppings, flies may lay their eggs in its coat. The eggs hatch into maggots, which burrow through the fur into your rabbit's skin. Maggots produce poisons that can kill a rabbit. If you see any maggots on your rabbit's fur, remove them with tweezers immediately and then take your pet to the vet for a check-up.

Going away

It is important to plan ahead when you are going away, as you will have to find someone to look after your rabbit. A neighbour may be willing to feed your pet each day. Otherwise, it may be necessary to move your rabbit and its hutch to a friend's or relative's house. You could ask a boarding cattery, as these sometimes take other pets, or your vet may know someone who could help. It is very important that your rabbit is cared for properly while you are away.

Buy enough of everything to last while you are away. It's not just food that will be needed, but hay, straw and bedding, too.

Written instructions

It is important to leave clear instructions, so write these out like a diary. Make it clear when your rabbit will need food, what type of food and how much will be required. This is especially important if your friend has never looked after a rabbit before.

Moving your rabbit

If you need to take your rabbit to a friend's house, do this a day or so before you go, and remember to pack everything to take with you. Transfer the rabbit to its carrier for the journey, and settle your pet in at its temporary home when you arrive. You can also answer any questions that your friend may want to ask, about how to look after your rabbit.

Move your rabbit in a special carrier rather than in its hutch. If you have to use a cardboard box, make sure that it will support your pet's weight.

Fit and healthy

Rabbits rarely become ill, especially if they are kept clean and well-fed. But, depending on where you live, it may be a good idea to have your pet vaccinated against the diseases known as myxomatosis and VHD. Ask your vet for advice. Rabbits will die if they become ill with either of these infections.

Varieties with long coats, such as a lionhead rabbit, will need more grooming than others.

Grooming tips

You do not need to spend a lot of time grooming a short-coated rabbit. You simply brush its coat gently, so that it is smooth.

Long-haired rabbits such as cashmere lops need more grooming than short-coated varieties. When grooming a long-haired rabbit brush the hair up and then comb it down again. This should be done about twice a week.

While grooming, you should also check your pet's eyes and ears. The eyes should be bright and not runny. Inside the ears should be free of scabs.

Signs of illness

If you think your rabbit is ill, contact your vet as quickly as possible. There are several likely signs of illness. Your pet may lose its appetite, it may have difficulty in eating its food, or its droppings may appear runnier than usual.

Teeth and claws

Check your pet's teeth, especially the incisors, as these can sometimes break. If the top and bottom sets do not meet properly, the rabbit will starve unless the teeth are trimmed regularly by your vet. The claws may also need to be cut back carefully, which you should ask your vet to do.

If your rabbit appears to be having any difficulty in eating, check its teeth. They could be overgrown or damaged.

This edition is published by Armadillo, an imprint of Anness Publishing Ltd,
Blaby Road, Wigston, Leicestershire LE18 4SE; info@anness.com

www.annesspublishing.com

If you like the images in this book and would like to investigate using them for publishing,
promotions or advertising, please visit our website www.practicalpictures.com for more information.

Publisher: Joanna Lorenz
Editor: Sarah Uttridge
Designer: Linda Penny
Photographer: Paul Bricknell
Production Controller: Pirong Wang

The publishers would like to thank Grace Crissell, Hannah Lie and Harry Grint for appearing
in this book. With special thanks to Chris Angell and Jill Wood for providing the rabbits.
Picture Credits: image on p3br courtesy of Stephen Rees/www.shutterstock.com; p10t courtesy of
Marilyn Barbone/www.shutterstock.com; p19tr courtesy of Dorottya Mathe/www.shutterstock.com.

PUBLISHER'S NOTE
Although the advice and information in this book are believed to be accurate and true at the time of
going to press, neither the authors nor the publisher can accept any legal responsibility or liability for any
errors or omissions that may have been made nor for any inaccuracies nor for any loss, harm or injury
that comes about from following instructions or advice in this book. If you are worried about your pet's
health, consult a veterinarian without delay.

Manufacturer: Anness Publishing Ltd, Blaby Road, Wigston, Leicestershire LE18 4SE, England
For Product Tracking go to: www.annesspublishing.com/tracking
Batch: 2739-22517-1127